# The Last Great World's Fair

## ❧ SAN FRANCISCO'S ❧

### PANAMA-PACIFIC INTERNATIONAL EXPOSITION 1915

Introduction by Hallie Brignall

Edited by Robert Lieber and Sarah Lau

Designed by Vivian Young

GOLDEN GATE NATIONAL PARKS CONSERVANCY

## ACKNOWLEDGEMENTS

The Parks Conservancy thanks Hallie Brignall, Susan Ewing-Haley, Marcus Combs, and Stephen Haller for their work and encouragement. We also appreciate the generosity of the Museum of American Heritage, Palo Alto; SFMuseum.net: The Virtual Museum of the City of San Francisco; the Maybeck Foundation; and Linden Hayes Fine Art, San Francisco.

ISBN 1-883869-88-9
Library of Congress Control Number: 2004100223

Photographs included in this book (with the exception of the Crissy Field photo on p.68) are part of the collection of the Park Archives and Records Center, Golden Gate National Recreation Area, and are used with permission.

This publication was produced in conjunction with the exhibit, "Panoramic Spectacle," on display February 20-April 18, 2004, at the Officers' Club in the Presidio of San Francisco. The exhibit was curated by Hallie Brignall and produced by the Golden Gate National Parks, the Golden Gate National Parks Conservancy, and the Presidio Trust.

Editors: Robert Lieber, Sarah Lau
Design: Vivian Young
Senior Editor: Susan Tasaki
Printed in the USA on recycled paper by The Printing Guys, San Francisco, CA

## GOLDEN GATE NATIONAL PARKS CONSERVANCY
*The Nonprofit Partner for the Golden Gate National Parks*

The Golden Gate National Parks Conservancy is a nonprofit membership organization created to preserve the Golden Gate National Parks, enhance the experiences of park visitors, and build a community dedicated to conserving the parks for the future.

# Hand-Tinted Photographs

# INTRODUCTION

Finding a passage between the Atlantic and Pacific oceans had been a dream of traders and mariners since the "discovery" of the Pacific by the Spanish explorer Vasco Nunez de Balboa in the sixteenth century. When the Panama Canal officially opened in 1914, it was hailed as a major achievement for the United States.

In anticipation of the canal's opening, numerous American cities vied for the right to host a world's fair celebrating this glorious achievement. In 1911, President Taft awarded the honor to San Francisco, and the city's businessmen set about creating an event that would not only commemorate this monumental feat, but also, the resurrection of their city from the devastating earthquake and fire of 1906.

By February 20, 1915, when the Panama-Pacific International Exposition officially opened, San Francisco's northern bayshore, including part of the Presidio and acres of wandering salt marsh, had been transformed into a magical city. Colorful buildings, original sculptures, and grand courts surrounded by lush, exotic landscaping proclaimed the power of human ingenuity. At the Exposition, beauty, science, philosophy, art, and industry converged to create a temporary but impressive display intended to enlighten and entertain as well as attract business and settlers to San Francisco. By the time the Exposition closed on December 4, almost 20 million people had explored its wonders.

Innumerable trinkets, postcards, and books were produced as souvenirs for the fair's visitors. Some of this ephemera was lovingly preserved in family collections, and later, given to local archives. The original version of this album, *Views of the Panama-Pacific International Exposition in Natural Colors,*\* now resides in the archives of the Golden Gate National Parks, which granted permission for its reproduction in a slightly more modern format in conjunction with the 2004 exhibition, "Panoramic Spectacle." The hand-tinted photographs and captions follow the original, with minor editorial alterations for consistency and readability. Further, the book was enriched with additional information that reveals more of the Exposition's incredible story.

Today, much as during the fair, the Marina and the Presidio are enjoyed by thousands of locals and visitors. Walk along the Golden Gate Promenade past the flat, grassy field that during the Exposition buzzed with the whine of race-car engines, and later (after the fair closed), with the roar of army biplanes; and past the tidal marsh, a suggestion of the rich wetlands that were filled in for the fair. Admire the classical frieze that supports the rotunda of the Palace of Fine Arts, and imagine a skyline filled with colorful buildings and extraordinary art. Perhaps also imagine yourself among the ladies and gentlemen strolling near the Tower of Jewels or sitting on a bench on the Avenue of Palms. San Francisco's hopes and dreams for a bright future were laid out for the world to see at the Exposition—step back into the city's cultural past on the pages of this album and discover what they experienced.

*Hallie Brignall*

\*Presidio Army Museum Records, GOGA-1766, Golden Gate National Recreation Area

# Panama Canal

On January 1, 1880, at the mouth of the Rio Grande, the first shovel of sand was dug and the Panama Canal was symbolically begun. The United States' interest in the Latin American canal peaked during the Spanish-American War of 1898, when the navy was unable to get the battleship *Oregon* to the Atlantic Ocean without a lengthy journey around the southern tip of South America. The 1903 Hay-Bunau-Varilla Treaty with the newly formed nation of Panama transferred the treacherous tasks of finishing France's construction of the Panama Canal and obtaining all rights to it to the United States.

The canal was officially opened on August 15, 1914, by the passing of the SS *Ancon* through its locks. Between 1904 and 1914, it was the most costly expenditure in American history, totaling $352,000,000. Combined with the French investment, expenditures totaled $639,000,000. In the 34 years it took to actually open the canal, it is estimated that over 80,000 people took part in the construction, and over 30,000 French and American lives were lost. The creation of the Panama Canal was significant for San Franciscans and the United States as a whole. In controlling the canal, the United States gained advantages in both war and trade, thus securing its position as a major world power.

COLONNADE OF THE PALACE OF FINE ARTS

This palace is entirely of steel and concrete for the safe keeping of the art treasures exhibited here. The architect, Bernard H. Maybeck, has so designed the palace that from every viewpoint it appears embowered. Wide terraces at the entrance level have tall trees on them planted close to the building, and tasteful arrangements of shrubbery surround these. Myrtles and roses are trained against the colonnades and a few cypresses are placed so that they contribute to the effect of repose sought here.

## Definition of a World's fair

The Industrial revolution of the late 19th and early 20th century sparked development of world's fairs into astounding competitive spectacles showcasing the advancement of civilization through invention, material wealth, and art. They brought prestige to the host country and its great cities, and were often invaluable in establishing future business prospects. Some of the most spectacular and memorable world's fairs were held in England (1851), France (1889), Chicago (1893), and St. Louis (1904).

Who came up with the idea of hosting a world's fair in San Francisco? Ruben Hale, founder of the Hale department stores, is credited with proposing to the directors of the city's Merchant Association as early as 1904 that San Francisco put itself forward as a host city.

THE ROTUNDA, PALACE OF FINE ARTS
This palace is recognized as perhaps the most beautiful individual building in an exposition that has become world-famous for its architecture, coloring, and lighting. Here we see how clearly the detail and coloring are revealed at night and how wonderfully pleasing are the reflections in the lagoon that surrounds the palace. The rotunda is 162 feet high.

## San Francisco, 1915: The Coast Metropolis

San Francisco has 360 miles of paved streets; 315.4 miles of sewers; and 278.58 miles of street railway lines, on many of which cars run all night. Any part of the city can be reached for a 5-cent fare. San Francisco is somewhat hilly, and its heights afford different vistas of the most delightful scenery surrounding any city in the world. Its bay rivals that of Naples, and the Golden Gate leading into it was so named from its resemblance to Constantinople's Golden Horn.

Population, 530,000, estimate of public service corporations.

Population of bay district, within twenty-mile radius of city hall, over 750,000. (This is the future Greater San Francisco, fourth city in size in the United States.)

Population per square mile, 9,947.5.

At Market and Fourth streets 19,106 vehicles were counted passing in a single business day, of which 3,826 were electric cars.

The Chinese quarter is the largest in the United States. Population, 11,000.

San Francisco has the largest shipbuilding plants on the Pacific Coast.

There are 156 daily, weekly, and monthly publications, embracing all languages.

There are 110 public and 26 private schools in the city of San Francisco.

San Francisco had 103,462 telephones on July 1, 1913, one to every five inhabitants, which is a larger ratio than that of any other large city in the world having one telephone system.

There were 1,795 manufacturing establishments in San Francisco according to the U.S. census of 1909.

Salaries and wages, $30,452,000 per year.

The largest fruit and vegetable cannery in the world is located in San Francisco.

*From 1915 pamphlet,* Facts About San Francisco, *published by the San Francisco Chamber of Commerce*

COURT OF ABUNDANCE

This court is architecturally a composite of many influences and has features that are entirely different from what is seen elsewhere in the Exposition. The influence of the late Renaissance is seen in the regular and formal plan of the court; of the Spanish in the general lines; and in the detail, a subtle strain of the Oriental.

It is here that the celebrated Brangwyn Murals are to be seen. There are eight canvases from the brush of that world-master. The landscape features are also distinctive. Orange trees laden with fruit are used in large numbers.

## Come to the Fair!

*Think of some of the glories that await you at the end of the golden trail:*

An expenditure of fifty million dollars in construction.

Fifty millions more in the intrinsic value of exhibitions.

Six hundred and twenty-five acres of Palaces and gardens entrancingly beautiful.

Eleven great Exhibit Palaces crowded with objects of interest from every portion of the globe.

Spacious courts and miles on miles of ornamented avenues.

More than two hundred and fifty groups of statuary by world's masters.

Huge mural paintings, masterpieces by the greatest artists.

An art palace, the architecture of which is more beautiful than any part of ancient Greece, and which contains the largest and most comprehensive collection of pictures ever collected and shown in one place.

Near two score Pavilions of the States and Foreign Nations vying with each other in architecture, displays, and hospitality.

Sixty-five acres of amusement concessions, several of which cost $250,000 to build.

An Aviation Field for the contest of the air and athletic sports.

A Drill Ground, where ten thousand troops may drill at one time.

A Livestock Exhibit embracing the entire world's best birds and animals.

An electrical illumination at night absolutely unique and unequaled.

*From The Virtual Museum of the City of San Francisco*

TOWER OF JEWELS SHOWING PALACE OF MANUFACTURES AT RIGHT AND PALACE OF LIBERAL ARTS AT LEFT
On the left of this picture may be seen the southern façade of the Palace of Liberal Arts, while the façade of the Palace of Manufactures in shown on the right. This is a general view along the Avenue of Palms, and across the great South Gardens from Festival Hall.

## Before the Fair Began

Due to high unemployment—which meant that more people had free time—and natural curiosity, large numbers of the San Francisco public went to the construction site to view the progress of the fair. At first, management did not consider charging these inquisitive observers, but over time the construction grounds became littered with flammable materials, especially cigarette butts. Fair management was quick to realize the extreme high risk of fire and other dangers as building structures rose higher and higher. To reduce the number of visitors, an admission policy was put in place on September 9, 1913. To be admitted into the construction ground to view its progress, the general public had to pay 25 cents per adult, 10 cents per child, and 50 cents per automobile. Each day, as many as 50,000 people purchased tickets to watch the progress of the fair's construction. The fair collected almost a quarter of a million dollars ($223,744.25) before the official opening day of February 20, 1915.

THE TOWER OF JEWELS AND CENTRAL EXHIBIT PALACES ILLUMINATED Perhaps the most attractive and beautiful general features of the Exposition are its electrical illuminations, and this picture gives but a faint idea of the wonderful flood of light that reveals by night the general grandeur as well as the minutest details of this great creation, and the exquisite color scheme so greatly admired by all is even more effective than when seen by daylight. At a point on the bay shore is erected an apparatus that weaves in the night sky auroras of ever-changing color, creating a wonderful and never-to-be forgotten spectacle.

## Opening Day

On February 20, 1915, an estimated 150,000 people, including Mayor James Rolph and Governor Hiram Johnson, paraded into the Fillmore Street Entrance. The throngs, who were required to pay for opening day badges even if they had already purchased season tickets, gathered inside the gates for opening ceremonies. After several speeches amidst a boisterous crowd, Exposition president Charles C. Moore made the first official transcontinental phone call to the President of the United States, Woodrow Wilson, 3,000 miles away, Wilson opened up Exposition hall doors and started fountains with the turn of a golden key. On cue, celebrated stunt pilot Lincoln Beachey flew overhead, performing tricks while releasing four white doves. Embracing new technology, the magical fair that had captured the popular imagination for more than a decade was officially opened.

WESTERN ENTRANCE, PALACE OF LIBERAL ARTS, FROM COURT OF PALMS

This view shows the wonderfully ornate entrance to the Palace of Liberal Arts. Liberal arts rank high in the classifications of exhibits because they embrace the applied sciences, which indicate the result of human education and culture. This splendid palace is directly opposite the main entrance to the exposition grounds from the city side and covers nearly 6 acres.

## San Francisco Welcomes the World

Construction of the Panama-Pacific International Exposition began in 1912. When the fair opened on Washington's Birthday, February 20, 1915, it covered 625 acres, was built within budget and on time, and broke all early attendance records.

Opening-day attendance: 255,149.

Opening-week attendance (February 20 to February 26): 659,000.

US population in 1915: 100,546,000; world population in 1915: 1,821,000,000.

Over 280,000 photographic permits were issued at $1 each.

Lowest attendance was the week of April 24-April 30: 285,580.

Highest attendance was the week of November 27-December 3: 753,682.

On December 4, 1915, the Exposition's last day, 459,022 visitors set an attendance record.

Total admission: 18,876,438 people (20 times the population of San Francisco).

Total revenue: $4,715,523.05.

ADMISSIONS

Gate Hours: 7 AM to 11 PM

General Admission: Adult, 50 cents; Children, 25 cents

Special Admission: Saturday and Monday, 15 cents (child's ticket); School group of 20, 5 cents; Soldiers and Sailors in uniform, Free

FESTIVAL HALL, ACROSS THE GREAT SOUTH GARDENS
Festival Hall is built in the French Theatre-style of architecture, with one large and various minor domes and minarets, profusely decorated with statuary. The main hall contains seats for about 3,000 persons, and here is placed a huge pipe organ that is seventh in size in the world.

## A Week in San Francisco

Visitors to San Francisco in 1915 would pay $1.00 (and up) to let a room for one day. Meals would cost them about $7.00 a week. With the price of admission to the fair at $.50 per day and streetcar fare, a basic week in San Francisco during the PPIE could cost about $20. Visitors could reduce their expenses by renting rooms by the week or month. In 1915 the national annual income was $1,267, the price of a new car was $390, and the price of a new house, $3,395.

CLIMATE

"The coldest winter I ever spent was one summer in San Francisco."
*Attributed to Mark Twain*

"Do not come clad for a hot Eastern summer. Light overcoats and wraps are always in demand in the evening. From April to November umbrellas may safely be left at home." These hints, along with other cautionary information, informed out-of-town visitors about San Francisco's climate. Unlike its sunny southern California counterparts, San Francisco has a moderate climate and is often cold.

Lowest temperature ever officially recorded here, 29 above zero.

Average winter temperature, 51 degrees.

Average summer temperature, 59 degrees. Cool weather makes San Francisco the best city summer resort in the country.

San Francisco has more hours of sunshine yearly than Boston, New York, Philadelphia, Chicago, Pittsburgh, or St. Louis.

Snow has fallen but six times in the city's history.

San Franciscans are a music-loving people and have one of the best permanent symphony orchestras in the country.

FESTIVAL HALL AND TOWER OF JEWELS BY NIGHT These new lighting effects are accomplished in part by the double use of concealed searchlights. Two rays of unequal power shine from different angles, and these lighten the shadows and emphasize the higher lights of prominent lines. On the bayshore is placed a "scintillator," comprising half a hundred powerful searchlights manned by as many operators specially trained for the work. At night, when these powerful rays of light are sent forth with ever-changing rainbow colors over the buildings and into the fleecy clouds or fog banks, it is a spectacle entrancing to young and old alike and of which none grow tired.

## It Happened Here First

The Panama-Pacific International Exposition brought together the latest in technology and creativity. It was a fair of many firsts.

FIRST airplane to cross the Isthmus of Panama displayed.

FIRST international exposition at which public enjoyed airplane rides.

FIRST to remain open nine-and-a-half months straight (no seasonal closings).

FIRST to show steam pyrotechnics.

FIRST to use movies in its exploitation (marketing).

FIRST exposition to select the members of its Guard from honorably discharged United States soldiers, sailors, and marines.

FIRST to exhibit a million-volt electric transformer.

FIRST exposition ever opened by the wireless telegraph.

FIRST transcontinental telephony was demonstrated; the first transcontinental telephone conversation took place between President Wilson and President Moore of the exposition, during the Exposition year.

FIRST use of indirect lighting.

FIRST to use colored lighting (night-time illumination)— over 370 search lights and 500 open or unglazed projectors used.

FIRST periscope exhibited in the United States.

FIRST to have trackless streetcars (Fadgl trains).

FIRST to show an automobile assembly plant in operation.

FIRST $50 gold coin issued under authority of the US for this Exposition struck by the San Francisco Mint.

FIRST ceremonial planting of trees was employed to emphasize and commemorate great occasions.

FIRST to use moving pictures in an exposition.

PALACE OF MANUFACTURES
This view shows the Palace of Manufactures from the Avenue of Palms. It is 475 by 552 feet and was erected at a cost of $317,436 [in 21st-century dollars, about $5,478,555]. Within its walls, exhibit space has been allotted to four thousand exhibitors, who display, in elaborate booths, the finest fabrics and manufactured goods of every description.

## Special Days

During the 288 days of the Panama-Pacific International Exposition, specific days were dedicated to acknowledge their importance and attract visitors. Below are just a few of the numerous "special days" that attracted fair-goers.

Baked Potato Day

Raisin Day

Child Labor Day

Buddha's Day

Non-Smokers' Protective League Day

Order of Moose Day

Druids Golden Jubilee Day

Doll Day

B'Nai Brith Day

Shakespeare Day

Knights & Ladies Honor Day

Ripe Olive Day

Patriots' Day

Pioneer Mothers Day

Typographical Union Day

Roosevelt Day

Peace Day

Guatemala Coffee Day

THE PALACE OF LIBERAL ARTS AND TOWER OF JEWELS BY NIGHT

In an entirely new manner unity has been achieved in the lighting. It is called "flood lighting," and comes from concealed sources. It differs from "line lighting" in that it does not dazzle the eyes of the spectator, who sees warmly lighted sur- faces, façades, and towers rather than sharp lines and clusters of lights.

## Famous Visitors to the Fair

**Buffalo Bill Cody** (1846-1917) Buffalo hunter, US Army Scout, famous for touring his Wild West Show and creating the myth of the American West.

**Charlie Chaplin** (1889-1997) Great silent film director and star of *Limelight, The Great Dictator, City Lights,* and *Modern Times*.

**Eddie Rickenbacker** (1890-1973) World War I flying ace, father of commercial flight, racecar driver, and owner of the Indianapolis 500 Speedway.

**Franklin Delano Roosevelt** (1882-1945) President of the United States between 1932 and 1945; this enormously popular "New Deal" president, whose terms spanned the Great Depression and WWII, was elected four times.

**Helen Keller** (1880-1968) Inspirational blind and deaf woman who became a role model for millions.

**Henry Ford** (1863-1947) Inventor of the Model-T and the practice of mass production of the automobile.

**John Philip Sousa** (1854-1932) Dubbed the "March King," he wrote The Stars and Stripes Forever.

**Laura Ingalls Wilder** (1867-1957) American pioneer and author of the famous "Little House on the Prairie" books.

**Mabel Normand** (1892-1930) Actress known as "The Queen of Comedy"; played a key role in the development of American film comedy.

**Maria Montessori** (1870-1952) Famous children's educator dedicated to the principle that "children teach themselves."

**William Howard Taft** (1857-1930) Twenty-seventh president of the United States (1909-1913).

**Theodore Roosevelt** (1858-1919) Twenty-sixth president of the United States (1901-1909), Instrumental in the creation of the National Park Service.

**Thomas Edison** (1847-1931) Inventor of the first electric light, electric distribution company, the phonograph, and more.

**Ansel Adams** (1902-1984) San Francisco photographer and environmentalist renowned for his photos of the landscape and America's national parks.

TOWER OF JEWELS FROM GREAT SOUTH GARDENS

This is a most pleasing view from Festival Hall, across the great South Gardens, embracing the Tower of Jewels and the Palace of Horticulture.

## Women and Morality

Women held over 114 conventions at the Panama-Pacific International Exposition. Convention subjects included religion; missions; suffrage; peace; child welfare; social hygiene; social economy; and governmental, fraternal, and professional interests. There were 2,160 women delegates from 39 states and 8 foreign countries. Some of the more well-known women included Mrs. Philip Snowden (wife of England's Labor leader), Miss Jane Addams (Hull House, Chicago), Mrs. Kate Waller Barrett (US Immigration Department), Madam Montessori, Madame Chen Chi (wife of the Chinese Commissioner General of the Exposition), Mrs. Ella Flagg Young (Chicago's Superintendent of Schools), Mrs. Phoebe A. Hearst, Mrs. Andreas Hofer Proudfoot, and Madam Ali-Kuli Khan.

MORAL PROTECTION

Dangers to unaccompanied women at the Chicago Exposition led PPIE officials (spearheaded by women's organizations) to take extra precautions in tending to their female out-of-town guests. They formed a Travelers Aid Society that assisted young women from the moment they arrived. Women were met as they got off trains and personally escorted to reputable lodgings. A clubhouse built in the Zone provided meals, baths, nurses, a sewing machine, and classes to help fair workers improve their employment skills. If a woman had reason to leave, the  club would assist her with transportation in getting home.

COURT OF THE UNIVERSE, LOOKING TOWARD ARCH OF THE RISING SUN

This is the great central court of honor of the exposition, and in design and decoration it is made to represent the meeting place of the hemispheres. It is 700 feet long and 900 feet wide, and contains a sunken garden in the center. In the center of the picture is the Fountain of the Setting Sun, while a little to the right is the Fountain of the Rising Sun. Surmounting the fountains on great globes symbolizing a Sunset and Sunburst, respectively, are beautiful winged figures. At night, the columns and globes give forth an incandescent glow, while below in the basins, reclining figures of the planets surmount globes of light behind which the water falls in screens.

## What to Wear to the Fair

In 1915, a classic dark suit of velvet or wool was proper attire for any woman stepping out in public; the outfit might have been described as follows:

Silhouette: Slim, high round bust, high waist, and narrow skirt.

Bodice: Fitted, worn over long-line corset.

Neckline: High, round, boat-shaped, square.

Sleeves: Long fitted, short dolman.

Skirt: Ankle-length, narrow

Fabric: Silk, wool, crepe-de-chine, silk georgette, silk jersey.

Trimmings: Braid, ribbon, fur, monkey fur, fringing, embroidery, beading.

Color: Bright, unusual color combinations.

Accessories: Large hats with wide brims and crowns, muffs, long gloves, bags, silk stockings; shoes with pointed toes, bar straps, and low Louis heels; large parasols, long-handled umbrellas.

*From the Museum of American Heritage*

THE PALACE OF HORTICULTURE AND PART OF THE GREAT SOUTH GARDENS
This beautiful structure from the plans of Bakewell and Brown is the largest and most splendid of the garden structures. Its dimensions are 672 by 320 feet, and its great dome—160 feet high and 152 feet in diameter—is larger than St. Peter's at Rome. It is constructed almost entirely of glass and at night is illuminated from within by means of a dozen huge searchlights. Mounted on the ground under the dome, they send their rays through screens of many colors, making the glass dome glow like a fire opal.

## Audrey Munson

Born in 1891, Audrey Munson saw her career peak when she was dubbed "The Exposition Girl" and "Miss Panama" in 1915 after having posed for 80 percent of the PPIE's sculptures and murals. As a result of her popularity, she had a brief career in film, becoming the first woman to shed her clothes on-screen in the film *Inspiration*. In 1919, Audrey was linked to a scandal involving murder and betrayal when her former landlord admitted to murdering his wife over an obsession with the young Audrey. She received further bad publicity when the press labeled her purported engagement and suicide attempt as "a calculated ruse to generate cheap publicity." Audrey never recovered from this notoriety and by 1931, her mental health was in serious question. At age 39, Audrey Munson entered a psychiatric institution, where she spent the next 65 years until her death in 1996 at the age of 105.

NICHE IN THE COURT OF THE UNIVERSE

Showing a corner of the Palace of Transportation and an entrance to the sunken gardens, luxuriant with tropical plants and flowers and pools reflecting the façades of the surrounding palaces. The Palace of Transportation is 618 feet long and 579 feet wide and cost $451,560 [in 21st-century dollars, about $7,793,374] for its erection. The exhibits are contemporaneous rather than historical. The very latest achievements of human ingenuity covering the entire field of transportation are displayed.

## The Zone: Amusements and Concessions

The amusement and concession part of the Exposition was called the Zone or "Playland." The Zone covered 65 acres (from Laguna Street to Van Ness Avenue). When the Zone was finally realized, its surprising building features and wonderfully inventive constructions created an area far more compelling than any amusement park. Large-scale dioramas and gigantic models astounded the public. Grand Canyon and Yellowstone National Parks, Japan Beautiful, and the Panama Canal were among the extraordinary and enormous models the visitor encountered.

The 455 concessions at the Zone varied widely, and at first its exhibitors were unhappy because business was poor. To arouse public appreciation for this unusual area, a committee of Zone showmen selected May 27 as "Zone Day" and staged a large-scale carnival. Despite the economic depression and the specter of a world war, the carnival was received with tremendous excitement. The Zone became the "happiest place on earth." The carnival proved to be a strong public attraction, increasing fair attendance more than two-fold as compared to the previous day and the day following.

Concessions at the fair were found in the Zone and included Heinz 57, Underwood Typewriter, Gillette Safety Razor, Sunmaid Raisins, MJB Coffee, Ford Motors, Southern Pacific, Snowflake Marshmallow Cream, Yellowstone National Park, Inside Inn, Desmond Supply Company, and YMCA Cafeteria.

PALM AVENUE, LOOKING TOWARD TOWER OF JEWELS Palm Avenue is the main thoroughfare between the great South Gardens and the group of main exhibit palaces. Beautiful California palms line either side of this avenue. On the right is seen the entrance to the Palace of Varied Industries, following which are two Italian Towers rising to a height of 200 feet, one at each side of the entrance to the Court of Flowers.

## Pan-Pacific Cookbook

The official cookbook of the Panama-Pacific International Exposition included international dishes representing the fair's diverse cuisine. Following is a sampling from the hundreds of recipes included in the book.

### Crab Soup-San Franciscan

Pound a cup of shredded crab meat and all the fat, reserving the meat from the claws, with half a cup of rice boiled until soft; moisten with cream and rub through a sieve into a pint of veal or chicken broth; simmer for fifteen minutes, then add a pint of scalding hot cream and the pieces of crab, a pinch of paprika and serve. A pint of milk scalded with an onion, bay leaf, and cloves, then strained, can be used instead of the stock.

### Canapé a l'Exposition

Fry six thin rounds of bread. Chop three tablespoons of cold chicken or ham and two anchovies, and pound to a paste. Add a tablespoon of thick cream and season with chili powder. Then spread on the toast. Sprinkle with grated cheese and brown in the oven.

### Ciopino-Neapolitan

Chop two onions and half a clove of garlic fine, with two branches of parsley and a stick of celery, and fry until yellow in a half a cup of olive oil; add a can of tomatoes and a cup of white wine and boil for half an hour; add two pounds of fish, cut into large portions (using several kinds), half a pound of scrubbed clams or mussels, and a boiled crab (with outside shell removed) broken into pieces. Season highly with salt and paprika and simmer until the fish are done. Pour over toasted French bread in a large, deep platter.

*From* Pan-Pacific Cookbook: Savory Bits from the World's Fare *by L. L. McLaren*

HALF DOME, COURT OF FOUR SEASONS, BY NIGHT

This picture gives a further idea of the beautiful lighting effects, particularly when the objects are reflected in one of the small lakes or lagoons. The reflections here portrayed are but one of scores of unsurpassed fairy pictures that may be seen any night by strolling around the grounds. Concealed batteries project powerful yet softened rays of light, revealing in wonderful clearness the façades and walls of the palaces and the natural colors of the shrubbery and flowers.

## World War I

What became known as "the Great War" began on August 14, 1914, less than a year before the Panama-Pacific International Exposition was set to open. European nations had been living with the threat of war long before the actual outbreak of hostilities, however, and this influenced their participation in the Exposition. Great Britain did not officially take part in the Exposition, and though German businessmen made some fine exhibits, there was no official German presence either.

The PPIE hosted several peace-themed events, including two women's peace conferences, a "Peace Day," an anti-war speech by William Jennings Bryan, a Pageant of Peace, and "the world's greatest peace play," *The Trojan Women.*

The US military played an important role in the PPIE. Half of the land used by the fair was leased from Presidio, and invitations were sent out to cadets all over the United States to participate. Soldiers served as guards, escorts for celebrities and dignitaries, and operators of the "scintillator "(colorful spotlights used to illuminate the fair at night); they also marched during celebrations, played music, and provided demonstrations of munitions and naval power.

TOWER OF JEWELS ACROSS THE GREAT SOUTH GARDENS Designed by Messrs. Carrere and Hastings of New York, this beautiful tower rises to a height of 433 feet, and from an architectural standpoint is the dominating feature of the exposition. The center of brilliant night illumination, the tower is defined by over 100,000 hand-cut glass jewels, which scintillate in a thousand different tints and colors.

## International Exhibitors

The Panama-Pacific International Exposition was truly an international affair. Thirty-one countries from around the globe were represented, twenty-five countries officially and six, unofficially. Twenty-three built exceptional pavilions in which they exhibited the best of their arts, industries, and resources. Among the multitude of objects on display were paintings, maps, and dioramas of their land, cities, rivers and harbors; mementoes of their history; and portraits of their living statesmen and illustrious dead.

In addition to putting the achievements of the world's nations on display, the PPIE was also the venue for a small and informal international congress. Interest in relations among nations was high, and at the PPIE, commissioners of various countries came together in propitious surroundings. Here, they heard one another's views and sentiments and exchanged expressions of good will.

COUNTRIES WITH PAVILIONS:

Argentina, Australia, Bolivia, Canada, China, Cuba, Denmark, France, Greece, Guatemala, Hawaii, Honduras, Italy, Japan, Netherlands, New Zealand, Norway, Panama, Philippine Islands, Portugal, Siam, Sweden, Turkey

COUNTRIES EXHIBITING ONLY:

Austria, Balkan states, Germany, Great Britain, India, Luxembourg, Mexico, Morocco, Persia, Russia, Spain, Switzerland, Uruguay

AVENUE OF PROGRESS

The Avenue of Progress leads from the Fillmore Street entrance, past the Service Building, the Palaces of Varied Industries and Mines and Metallurgy on the left, and the Palace of Machinery on the right, to the Marina. This avenue is at the extreme eastern border of the main group of exhibit palaces. The Palace of Machinery (on the right of the picture) is the largest individual building in the exposition, and indeed is the largest wooden frame building in the world, at 967 feet in length by 367 feet in width and 121 feet in height. Over 8,000,000 feet of lumber and 1,500 tons of steel bolts and washers were used in its construction. It covers approximately 9 acres of floor space.

## The World in Motion Pictures

The development of the motion picture gave the fair an advantage over its predecessors. In addition to the products exhibited by different international exhibitors, films were used to show the countries themselves—their topography, transportation systems, harbors, mines, and life and industries. Films were also used to show how the exhibited products were produced, and the working conditions of the people responsible for these products.

*Sampling of Items Exhibited by Foreign Countries*

GUATEMALA
Oats, wheat, barley, rice, corn, rubber, cocoa, coffee, basketry, embroidery, cigars, tobacco, taxidermy, nuts, seeds, oils, sugar, artificial limbs, guitars, ore, vegetable dye, wool, timber, bananas.

GREECE
Sculpture, textiles, fruits, wines, nuts, olives, olive oil, currants, tobacco, perfumes, silk, wool, cotton, rugs, embroidery, laces, iron, copper ore, magnetite fire brick, honey, raisins, saffron, almonds, walnuts, pepper, alfalfa, liquor, soap, cosmetics

AUSTRALIA
Rare birds, kangaroos, wallabies, paddy melons, wool, fruit, jam, wheat, oats, barley, corn, frozen meat, cordage, saddlery, mohair, hides, bones, glue, butter, cheese, coffee, rubber, indigo, cotton, eucalypts, jarrah, karri, mahogany, red bean rosewood

SIAM (Thailand)
Rice, timber, cotton, oils, gums, silks, rubber, tobacco, dyes, tannin, spices, handicrafts, ore, embroidery, porcelain, plumage of tropical birds, ivory, weaponry, fans, parasols

A VIEW IN THE GREAT SOUTH GARDEN
The great South Garden, 3,000 feet in length, is a marvel of landscape engineering skill, and reflects the transformation that has taken place on the grounds under the direction of John McLaren, who was chiefly responsible for this important work. The frostless climate of San Francisco has permitted plants and shrubbery and semi-tropical trees to attain the highest perfection even through the winter months, and it is hard to believe that a scene such as this has been created within the space of one short year.

## Words of Wisdom from Around the World

Inscriptions were found throughout the Exposition. Below is a partial collection from the Arches of the Court of the Universe, the largest of the courts in the Exposition and a symbolic meeting place of the Eastern and Western Hemispheres.

AMERICA: Facing West from California's shores—inquiring tireless seeking what is yet unfound—I a child very old over waves toward the house of maternity the land of migrations look afar—look off the shores of my Western sea the circle almost circled. *Whitman*

ARABIA: He who honors not himself lacks honor wherever he goes. *Zuhayr*

CHINA: They who know the truth are not equal to those who love it. *Confucius*

ITALY: The world is in its most excellent state when justice is supreme. *Dante*

FRANCE: The Universe—an infinite sphere, the center everywhere, the circumference nowhere. *Pascal*

GERMANY: It is absolutely indispensable for the Untied States to effect a passage from the Mexican Gulf to the Pacific Ocean and I am certain that they will do it. Would that I might live to see it, but I shall not. *Goethe*

INDIA: The moon sinks yonder in the West while in the East the glorious sun behind the herald dawn appears—Thus rise and set in constant change those shining orbs and regulate the very life of this our world. *Kalidasa*

JAPAN: Our eyes and hearts uplifted seem to gaze on heaven's radiance. *Hitomaro*

PERSIA: The balmy air diffuses health and fragrance—so tempered is the genial glow that we know neither heat nor cold-tulips and hyacinths abound—fostered by a delicious clime the earth blooms like a garden. *Firdausi*

SPAIN: Truth—Witness of the past, councilor of the present, guide of the future. *Cervantes*

THE TOWER OF JEWELS FROM THE SOUTH

The height of this great tower can hardly be realized from the picture. It is 433 feet high and has a vaulted base 110 feet high and 60 feet wide, through which entrance is had to the Court of the Universe. Above the great columns on either side of the archway are four figures by John Flanagan: the Soldier, the Priest, the Philosopher, and the Adventurer-moving types of the Renaissance. The first terrace is ornamented by repetitions of an armored horseman by F. M. L. Tonetti, typifying the Spanish explorer of the sixteenth century. Within the archway are canvases by William De Leftwich, commemorating the completion of the Panama-Pacific Canal.

## Preserving the Palace of Fine Arts

"There is always agitation about preserving the Exposition and keeping it open indefinitely during the closing months of every such affair. There always is and it is always futile. An Exposition is not a thing that can be sustained indefinitely. It is a beautiful rocket that will not stay up long, and there is little joy in playing with the stick. It is a thing of sentiment and emotion, and those are psychic fires that burn themselves out." Frank Morton Todd, *The Story of the Exposition.*

When the fair closed—with the exception of the Palace of Fine Arts, the California Building, and the Marina with the Columns of Progress as its dominating feature—its buildings needed to go. Fair items in general were priced at about 50 percent of what they had cost. In some instances, the price was higher and in others, far lower because of deterioration; none of the PPIE's structures had been intended to be permanent.

Preservation work went forward in an effort to save the Palace of Fine Arts, the Marina, the Column of Progress, and the California Building. Real estate needed to be purchased and funds raised to retrofit these ephemeral structures. Additionally, the Palace of Fine Arts required operating funds. The Exposition Preservation League, the San Francisco Art Association, many citizen organizations of San Francisco, the State Commission, and the Trustees of San Francisco State Normal School busily set to the work of fundraising.

Intended to generate enough money to allow the Palace of Fine Arts to remain open another year, the Artists' Ball, held on April 29, 1916, was one of the League's last hurrahs. Thousands walked and drove to the California Building through the wreckage of the Exposition palaces, a desolation oddly illuminated by the few remaining searchlights. The event raised about $3,000 toward the $30,000 needed to operate the Palace of Fine Arts for a year. Since the Art Association had already raised $23,000, the Exposition turned over the building. During its first five months of operation, attendance at the Palace of Fine Arts ran an encouraging 400 people a day.

PALACE OF FINE ARTS
At the west end of the central block, the Palace of Fine Arts is one of the delights of the wonder city. It is semicircular in form and faces a natural lagoon embowered in shrubbery and flowers, whose waters have been appropriated by wild ducks. Its length from north to south describes an arc of 1,100 feet. In the center of the arc is erected a great dome with steps leading down to the lagoon in the beautiful setting of Monterey cypress and other evergreen trees. Reflected in the placid waters of the lagoon, it is the prettiest vista of the whole Exposition site.

## National Parks at the Fair

At the Panama-Pacific International Exposition, visitors were treated to large-scale reproductions of the Grand Canyon and Yellowstone national parks. Located in the Zone, these displays showed off the natural beauty and variation of the United States landscape, encouraging visitation and support of further conservation. One year later, President Woodrow Wilson created the National Park Service to "protect and preserve" lands deemed irreplaceable parts of the nation's heritage. A young visitor to the fair named Ansel Adams would later be celebrated as one of the premier photographers of many national parks.

In 1994, the Presidio of San Francisco, which provided land for much of the western end of the fairgrounds, became part of the National Park System and one of the sites within the Golden Gate National Recreation Area. Today, the Presidio, including the magnificent coastal park Crissy Field, is under the cooperative protection of the Presidio Trust and Golden Gate National Recreation Area.

ARCHES OF THE RISING SUN AND THE SETTING SUN
The Court of the Universe in size and general scale dominates all the other courts in the Exposition. It is entered from the east and from the west through two massive triumphal arches surmounted by statuary groups representing the Spirit of the East and the Spirit of the West, respectively. This picture shows the view from the Arch of the Rising Sun, with that of the Setting Sun in the distance. McKim, Mead and White of New York designed the court, and the statuary groups are by A. Stirling Calder.

## Architecture and the Architects

The smoked ivory-tone artificial travertine was chosen for the buildings and all the statuary at the fair. Real travertine, which is abundant in Tivoli, Italy, is a form of calcium carbonate, a creamy-white deposit formed by the water of springs or streams containing lime. Real travertine was used to build both the Coliseum and St. Peter's in Rome.

PPIE buildings were covered with plastic travertine, made with Nevada gypsum combined with hemp fiber and a coloring pigment. Imitation tiles were used on the roofs of the buildings because real tiles were deemed too costly for this temporary "city."

Manager in Chief—George Kelham, San Francisco

Court of the Universe—McKim, Meade and White, New York

Tower of Jewels—Thomas Hastings, New York

Court of the Ages—Louis Christian Mullgardt, San Francisco

Court of the Four Seasons—Henry Bacon, New York

Courts of Flowers and Palms, the Italian Towers—George Kelham, San Francisco

Column of Progress—Symmes Richardson, New York

Palace of Machinery—Ward and Blohme, San Francisco

Palaces of Varied Industries, Mines, Manufactures, Transportation, Liberal Arts, Education, Agriculture, Food Products, and all portals and aisles—W. B. Faville, San Francisco

Palace of Fine Arts—Bernard Maybeck, San Francisco

Palace of Horticulture—Bakewell and Brown, San Francisco

Festival Hall—Robert Farquhar, Los Angeles

THE GREAT SOUTH GARDENS

In the South Gardens, the formal French treatment has been followed with most pleasing effect. To produce these effects, two years of preparatory work were necessary. Thousands of full-grown trees, from 20 to 50 feet in height, were boxed and moved to their new locations, and nearly 250,000 were raised in the Exposition nurseries. For the floral color effect, which, thanks to California's climate, will be continuous from February to December, three plantings will be necessary; for each of these, about 200,000 plants will have to be ready.

## Cost of Building a Palace

|  | 1915 | Current |
|---|---|---|
| Fine Arts and Annex | $631,929.29 | $10,906,311.78 |
| Education | 300,183.04 | 5,180,785.06 |
| Food Products | 326,594.69 | 5,636,617.22 |
| Liberal Arts | 325,447.90 | 5,616,825.05 |
| Agriculture | 386,351.48 | 6,667,994.92 |
| Manufactures | 317,436.35 | 5,478,555.68 |
| Transportation | 451,560.70 | 7,793,374.77 |
| Varied Industries | 296,554.07 | 5,118,153.56 |
| Mines and Metallurgy | 338,549.25 | 5,842,938.02 |
| Machinery | 655,336.35 | 11,310,288.46 |
| Horticulture | 352,615.90 | 6,085,710.86 |
| | $4,382,559.02 | $75,637,555.38 |

NORTHERN ENTRANCE TO THE COURT OF THE UNIVERSE
On the right may be seen the Palaces of Liberal Arts and Agriculture; on the left, the Palaces of Transportation and Manufactures. The Tower of Jewels is in the far distance, and the bandstand used for daily concerts is shown at the end of the lagoon.

## New York and State Buildings

In 1915, New York was the leading American state in terms of population and wealth. Using her extremely influential position, she threw her great congressional weight in support of San Francisco's bid to host the PPIE and in so doing, clinched the deal.

Most of the state buildings occupied the section of the grounds lying north of the Esplanade, along the edge of San Francisco Bay. The buildings were situated with magnificent views, and thousands of people visited their state's building to meet others from home, get their mail, read hometown papers, and rest on verandas and watching the big ships cruise in and out through the Golden Gate (*sans* bridge) to destinations around the globe.

PARTICIPATING STATES

Arkansas, California, Idaho, Illinois, Indiana, Iowa, Kansas, Maryland, Massachusetts, Missouri, Mississippi, Montana, Nevada, New Jersey, New York, North Dakota, Ohio, Oklahoma, Oregon, Pennsylvania, Texas, Utah, Virginia, Washington, West Virginia, Wisconsin

CALIFORNIA STATE BUILDING

This is the Host Building, and was erected by the citizens of the state from the plans of Thomas H. F. Burditte. It is, next to the Palace of Machinery, the largest building in the exposition and covers an area measuring 434 by 707 feet; it cost $655,336 [in 21st-century dollars, about $11,310,288] in construction and equipment. It contains the exhibits of the fifty-eight counties of the state. The Woman's Board has entire charge of the social administration of the building.

## General Financial Statement

RECEIPTS

Public Subscriptions $5,716,320

State of California Subscriptions $4,941,556

Municipal Aid, City & County of San Francisco $5,000,000

Mortgage Note Loan $1,112,500

Admission Revenue $4,983,610

Concession Revenue $1,599,360

Miscellaneous Income $2,884,257

Salvage $940,460

**TOTAL** $27,178,063

EXPENSES

Development and Construction $18,452,616

Operations & Maintenance $4,979,307

Mortgage Note Loan $1,112,500

Closure and Site Restoration $1,321,490

**TOTAL** $25,865,913

**Surplus $1,312,150**

PALACE OF TRANSPORTATION AND PALACE OF AGRICULTURE FROM THE WATERFRONT These two great exhibit palaces are on the Marina fronting San Francisco Bay, and what they lack in architectural ornamentation is more than made up for by their location. The view from the Marina, with its wide sweep of beautiful lawn across the island-dotted bay to the Marin hills on the other side and Mount Tamalpais in the rear, is one that is seldom equaled. From the yacht harbor, pleasure trips are to be had on the bay, and the passing ocean commerce is an added source of interest.

## Last Day and Night

It had rained heavily all the day before, but the morning of December 4, 1915, broke as fair as any day in midsummer, and by eleven o'clock the sun was burning in a cloudless California sky. From the Arches of the Rising and the Setting Sun, the colossal Nations of the East and Nations of the West looked down upon a multitude that could not have numbered less than 150,000 people. This was not a sad audience, but a satisfied and gratified one, for the work to which the city had set its hand had been completed to everyone's great satisfaction.

*From* The Story of the Exposition *(v. 5), by Frank Morgan Todd*

MULLGARDT'S TOWER AND COURT OF ABUNDANCE The Court of Abundance, designed by Louis C. Mullgardt, is the eastern-central court of the exposition, and in design shows the Oriental effect of the Spanish-Moorish type. This is dedicated to music, dancing, and pageantry.

## What Else Happened in 1915?

Europe is at war.

Woodrow Wilson is president of the United States.

Thomas Marshall is vice-president of the United States.

Albert Einstein develops his theory of relativity.

The British ship *Lusitania* is sunk.

Twenty-five thousand people march in suffrage parade in New York City.

The first telephone connection is made between the US and Japan.

The Boston Red Sox win the World Series.

Commercial air conditioning is introduced.

Eleanora Sears is the first woman to ride astride (rather than sidesaddle) at the National Horse Show.

First trans-Atlantic radiotelephone messages are sent.

Ford builds its one-millionth car.

FAMOUS PEOPLE IN THE ARTS BORN IN 1915

Saul Bellow (writer), Ingrid Bergman (actress), Yul Brynner (actor), Alice Faye (actress), Adolph Green (librettist), Billie Holiday (singer), Ring Lardner Jr. (writer), Anita Louise (writer), Arthur Miller (writer), Zero Mostel (actor), Les Paul (musician), Edith Piaf (singer), Anthony Quinn (actor), Ann Sheridan (actress), Frank Sinatra (singer), Elisabeth Schwarzkopf (opera singer), Robert Shaw (actor), Eli Wallach (actor), Muddy Waters (musician), Orson Wells (filmmaker), Herman Wolk (writer)

TOWER OF JEWELS AND STATUE, END OF THE TRAIL

This is a beautiful view looking from the Palace of Education and Social Economy toward the Tower of Jewels. The equestrian statue, *End of the Trail*, marks the entrance of the Court of Palms. The statue was designed by James Earl Fraser and is a remarkably realistic piece of work commanding general admiration.

## World's Fairs

| | |
|---|---|
| 1851 | London |
| 1853-54 | New York |
| 1855 | Paris |
| 1862 | London |
| 1867 | Paris |
| 1873 | Vienna |
| 1876 | Philadelphia |
| 1878 | Paris |
| 1889 | Paris |
| 1893 | Chicago |
| 1894 | San Francisco (California Midwinter International Exposition) |
| 1897 | Brussels |
| 1900 | Paris |
| 1904 | Saint Louis |
| 1910 | Brussels |
| 1913 | Gent |
| 1915 | San Francisco Panama-Pacific International Exposition |
| 1915 | San Diego, Panama-California Exposition (Unofficial) |
| 1924-25 | London (Wembley) |
| 1925 | Paris |
| 1926 | Philadelphia |
| 1929 | Seville and Barcelona |
| 1931 | Paris |
| 1933-34 | Chicago |
| 1935 | Brussels |
| 1937 | Paris |
| 1939-40 | New York |
| 1939-40 | San Francisco |
| 1958 | Brussels |
| 1962 | Seattle |
| 1964-65 | New York |
| 1967 | Montreal |
| 1970 | Osaka |
| 1974 | Spokane |
| 1982 | Knoxville |
| 1984 | New Orleans |
| 1985 | Tsukuba |
| 1986 | Vancouver |
| 1988 | Brisbane |
| 1992 | Seville |
| 1993 | Taejon |
| 1998 | Lisbon |
| 2000 | Hanover |

THE TOWER OF JEWELS ILLUMINATED

A flood of light sent forth by hundreds of searchlights from all directions makes the night scene at the Exposition one never to be forgotten. As these shafts of light strike the Main Tower, they cause tens of thousands of specially prepared glass "jewels," hung tremulously upon the tower, to flash and scintillate like great diamonds, emeralds, and rubies.

The night was balmy with hardly a breeze. The end was near. For years, most of those gathered had worked and waited and hoped for the Exposition. For 288 days it had celebrated the greatest material achievements in science, industry, and commerce, and in the appreciation of art.

## Jules Guerin: Chief of Color

On July 24, 1912, the eminent colorist Jules Guerin was appointed "Chief of Color" of the PPIE. Never before had one artist been given the power to direct the color scheme for an entire city. Jules Guerin's early work was connected with the theater, devising and painting for spectacular productions. He was the perfect person to take on this enormous challenge, creating an astounding visual world. It was one of the many remarkable achievements of the fair.

It was determined that the Exposition would not be the hard-marble tradition of other fairs, which was usually worked out in white plaster that by Closing Day had taken on a paste-board shabbiness. Guerin planned his color scheme to work with the strong light of California. Colors were well toned down and mellow. The colors were all in a high key, light and luminous. No matter what colors were next to each other there was only softness and tranquility. Guerin achieved a tonal scheme full of calm, peace, and beauty.

The shades used came to have their own designations. "Travertine," the base tint, a soft, pale buff, almost an ivory tint. It was the general background, and it glowed. The "dome green," between verdigris and Chinese jade, a shade much used in Asia, covered almost all the domes over the centers of the palaces. The "lattice green," which was used on doors, lattices, trellises of the Horticultural Palace, and some other structures, was a strong primary color, and it gave the portals a crisp distinction. Additionally, burnt orange was used on some of the domes.

Color was applied to domes, portals, tile roofs, columns, capitals, bases, moldings, aprons, backgrounds of friezes, walls in courts and behind colonnades, and all architectural ornament. It was applied to the statuary, flagpoles, benches, and even garbage cans. Pink sand for the walks was obtained by heating Monterey beach sand in a furnace to 600 degrees.

| | |
|---|---|
| Travertine | Pinkish red-gold |
| Gray | Wall-red |
| Yellow-golden orange | Pompeiian red |
| French green | Mud pink |
| Oxidized copper-green | Cerulean blue |
| Blue-green | Oriental blue |

## Aeroplane View of Main Group of Exhibit Palaces

This unusual and remarkable view is a reproduction of a photograph taken by Carl Wallen from the aeroplane of Silas Christofferson at an altitude of about 1,500 feet, and outlines clearly the general plan and arrangement of the main group of exhibit palaces, from the Palace of Machinery at the east to the Palace of Fine Arts at the west; the California State Building can be seen at the lower left-hand corner.

The exposition site combines to an unusual degree the qualities of beauty and adaptability; unity is the key note to its general plan, architecture, and color scheme. It nestles in a natural amphitheatre fronting on the world-renowned San Francisco Bay just inside the Golden Gate. It is flanked on the west by the eucalyptus-covered hills of the Presidio and on the east by Fort Mason; to the south rise steep hills covered with San Francisco homes. The view facing north across the sparkling waters of the bay and beyond is of the Marin hills crowned by Mt. Tamalpais.

For the exposition grounds, 625 acres in extent, the council of architects adopted a general plan that was as bold as it has proven successful. The units are not individual buildings but courts with intervening aisles and continuous façades. Approaching the exposition from the main entrance at the foot of Scott Street, the visitor enters the great South Gardens, 3,000 feet in length. On the right is the Festival Hall, while to the extreme left is the Palace of Horticulture. Immediately in front is the main tower of the Tower of Jewels. Passing under the arch of this great tower, the visitor enters the Court of the Universe, the largest of the five courts of the exposition. To the right, through the Triumphal Arch of the Rising Sun, is the Court of Abundance, which terminates at its southern extremity in the Court of Flowers, one of the minor courts.

To the left from the Court of the Universe, underneath the other Triumphal Arch, the visitor reaches the Court of the Four Seasons, which at its southern extremity enters the other minor court, the Court of Palms. Continuing straight ahead through the Court of Universe, one comes to the edge of the spacious Yacht Harbor and the center of the Grand Esplanade, or Marina. On the Marina, a wide sweep of lawn reaches from the north façade to the bay.

Instead of the work of the architects being divided into individual palaces, to one was designed the exterior walls of the entire group, with the great openings at the eight main gateways; W. V. Faville undertook this important work. To McKim, Mead and White were assigned the creation of the great central court, the Court of the Universe. This involved the treatment of portions of the exterior of four different palaces. The two other main courts were treated in the same way. Louis C. Mullgardt designed the Court of Abundance, while Henry Bacon was the architect of the Court of the Four Seasons and George W. Kellham has treated the great esplanades leading from the south into the Court of the Four Seasons.

In the central block in the exposition are eight great exhibit palaces devoted respectively to Food Products, Agriculture, Transportation, Mines and Metallurgy, Education and Social Economy, Liberal Arts, Manufactures, and Varied Industries, together with the Palace of Machinery at the east and the Palace of Fine Arts at the west, and the Palace of Horticulture and Festival Hall in the great South Gardens already referred to. Surmounting and dominating the design of this central block is the Tower of Jewels, designed by Carrere and Hastings and deriving its name from the fact that it glitters by day and night with 100,000 cleverly cut crystals with which it is studded.

West of the main exhibit buildings and east of the aviation field and drill grounds, a large area is devoted to the foreign nations, and states and territories of the United States. About forty foreign nations and forty-two states, territories, and possessions of the United States are officially represented at the exposition and have pavilions or buildings on the grounds.

To the east of the Palace of Machinery, 65 acres are devoted to the Zone—the amusement or concessions district—on which, it is estimated, more than $12,000,000 [in 21st-century dollars, about $218,495,000] has been expended.

This is the first exposition to have a uniform color scheme throughout. Not only has the whole color work been conceived by Jules Guerin as if the exposition were a single canvas, but the neutral browns and reds and yellows of the Marin hills in summer, with the marine blues and greens of the bay and ocean, have been blended in the composition of walls and domes and courts with singular success.

Photo: David Sanger

CRISSY FIELD:
A PLACE
TRANSFORMED

The Exposition spanned 625 acres, including much of the land known today as Crissy Field. This stretch of San Francisco shoreline continues to undergo many changes. In 2001, the National Park Service and its nonprofit partner, the Golden Gate National Parks Conservancy, completed a major restoration of the 100-acre site, transforming it into a spectacular national park at the center of the Golden Gate National Parks. As shown above, the Palace of Fine Arts is the only remaining building from the exposition. This graceful structure now welcomes visitors as it harkens back to the international panorama of nearly a century ago.

◀ FOLD OUT AERIAL VIEW

## Sources

Deitrick, Elizabeth Platt. *Best Bits of the Panama-Pacific International Exposition and San Francisco*. San Francisco: Galen Publishing Co., 1915.

Ewald, Donna, and Peter Clute. *San Francisco Invites the World: The Panama-Pacific International Exposition 1915*. San Francisco: Chronicle Books, 1991.

James, Juliet. *Palaces and Courts of the Exposition*. San Francisco: California Book Company, 1915.

Markwart, A. H. *Building an Exposition*. San Francisco: Panama-Pacific International Exposition, 1915.

McLaren, L. L. *Pan-Pacific Cook Book: Savory Bits from the World's Fare*. San Francisco: The Blair-Murdock Company, 1915.

Rozas, Diane, and Anita B. Gottehrer. *American Venus: The Extraordinary Life of Audrey Munson, Model and Muse*. Glendale, California: Balcony Press, 1999.

San Francisco Chamber of Commerce. *Facts About San Francisco, 1915*. Pamphlet archived at Park Archives and Records Center, National Park Service, GGNRA.

San Francisco Panama-Pacific International Exposition. *Condensed Facts Concerning the Exposition, 1915*. Archived at San Francisco Public Library, History Room.

Todd, Frank Morton. *The Story of the Exposition* (5 vol.). New York: The Knickerbocker Press, 1921.

## Golden Gate National Parks Conservancy

*The Nonprofit Partner for the Golden Gate National Parks*

The Golden Gate National Parks Conservancy is a nonprofit membership organization created to preserve the Golden Gate National Parks, enhance the experiences of park visitors, and build a community dedicated to conserving the parks for the future.

We seek private contributions to augment federal funds for the parks and work in collaboration with the National Park Service and the Presidio Trust to improve park sites, enlist volunteers in restoration projects, provide services and education programs for visitors and local communities, and engage diverse audiences in the national parks at the Golden Gate. To become a member or find out more, call (415) 4R-PARKS or visit *www.parksconservancy.org*.

## National Park Service
## Golden Gate National Parks

The National Park Service (NPS) was created in 1916 to preserve America's natural, cultural, and scenic treasures. The NPS manages the Golden Gate National Recreation Area (commonly known as the Golden Gate National Parks) as well as 387 other national parks sites across the country. For more information about the Golden Gate National Parks, call (415) 561-4700 or visit *www.nps.gov/goga*.

## The Presidio Trust

The Presidio Trust was created by Congress in 1996 to preserve and enhance the Presidio in partnership with the National Park Service. The Trust has jurisdiction over the interior 1,168 acres of the former military post. To learn more about the Presidio Trust, call (415) 561-5300, or visit *www.presidio.gov*.